Unto Us Is Born...

Unto Us Is Born...

Christmas Conversations with the Mother of Jesus

Herbert Brokering

Augsburg
MINNEAPOLIS

UNTO US IS BORN . . .
Christmas Conversations with the Mother of Jesus

Cover design: Craig Claeys
Interior design: Marti Naughton and Timothy W. Larson

Library of Congress Cataloging-in-Publication Data
Brokering, Herbert F.
   Unto us is born . . . : Christmas conversations with the mother of Jesus / Herbert Brokering.
      p. c.m.
   Includes bibliographical references.
   ISBN 0-8066-3897-4 (alk. paper)
   1. Advent Prayer-books and devotions—English. 2. Christmas Prayer-books and devotions—English. 3. Mary, Blessed Virgin, Saint—Motherhood.
4. Imaginary conversations. I. Title.
BV40.B75 1999   99-29517
242'.33—dc21   CIP

The paper used in this publication meets the minimum requirements of American National Standard for Information Sciences—Permanence of Paper for Printed Library Materials, ANSI Z329.48-1984.

Manufactured in the U.S.A.   AF 9-3897

03   02   01   00   99   1   2   3   4   5   6   7   8   9   10

To all who bear Christ

FOREWORD

*U*nto *Us Is Born* is a daily Christmas reader—a collection of my imaginary conversations with the mother of Jesus. Beginning December 1 and ending January 6, there are thirty-seven visits with the young woman who bore the Son of God.

The conversations grew out of images I have from Scripture, from classic nativity paintings, from years of childlike faith, from memories of my own mother.

Unto Us Is Born celebrates a mother and her child, celebrates all mothers and children. The child of Mary's hopes, dreams, and wonder was Jesus. That makes this mother's story very special.

For centuries, women before Mary hoped to bear the Savior. What did young Mary feel about so great a gift to her? How did this Jewish girl receive and act on the message of Archangel Gabriel? What did she see when she sang the old prayer named Magnificat? What did she say and feel about the child growing in her? What was in the world of Mary as the child grew within her?

Those were my questions. I offer Mary's answers in these readings. I let her speak to my mind, to my wondering. As I listen to Mary's soul, I feel the souls of all parents, caring about their children and caring about Mary's child.

Mary was deeply connected to her child through thoughts and feelings, in hopes, dreams, needs, fear, faith. The conversations with Mary speak of intimacy and faith within all families. My mother was close to me. She spoke softly to me of feelings, of dreams for me. We talked about destiny, want, fear, hope, faith. We talked about my name, about who I am, my gifts, the future. My mother made me special through tiny conversations.

In *Unto Us Is Born*, Mary sees her child as special. The conversations are not primarily about Mary; most of all they are about the child in her. She moves each conversation toward the wonder of her child, Jesus.

St. Francis of Assisi expressed a wish to be pregnant with Christ, to bear Christ as a mother bears a child, to spiritually birth the Son of God. The Carter Center in Atlanta has a painting of St. Francis holding the Christ child as though he were the child's mother: the Saint of Assisi as Madonna. In these thirty-seven conversations I often imagine myself to be Mary, with Christ inside me.

St. Francis is right: we can be pregnant with Christ. In these readings, everyone gets to be Mary. In real life, we all can carry Christ inside us.

Unto Us Is Born first appeared as a devotional booklet for Wheat Ridge Ministries. The Wheat Ridge focus on healing and hope inspired and guided these conversations. Mary's child was sent to make us well, to give us hope; Jesus came to save, to heal.

The ministry of Jesus was announced to Mary by the angel Gabriel. His name would be Jesus; he would save. The child would be both royal and servant. Every child is born to be royal and to serve. Mothers, fathers—parents everywhere—carry that dream in them for every infant born. Mary, the mother of Jesus, carries this eternal dream for all the world.

These thirty-seven conversations are designed for daily reading in the month of December and the first six days of January—through the seasons of Advent and Christmas. They may be read by one person, silently or aloud. And they may be read responsively as dialogues—by friends, by families, in small worship or discussion groups. I read them aloud as I wrote them. I read them quietly, wondering and reflecting. I read them reverently. I read them with delight. These readings mostly make me glad.

I can't recall when I didn't know the words "Mary kept all these things and pondered them in her heart." The conversations in this book are about Mary's pondering heart—and about our hearts. The child inside her is "Emmanuel," God with us. This book is about God with us: God in Mary, God in us; God with us, for us, through us. God born for us.

Unto us is born—unto *you* is born—a Savior who is Christ the Lord.

We get to carry the Christ child. Rejoice!

Herbert Brokering

A FORMAT FOR GROUP OR FAMILY ADVENT AND CHRISTMAS DEVOTIONS

LEADER: We gather to worship the Christ Child. We gather to ponder, with Mary, the wonder and mystery of his birth.

ALL: Be with us, Christ Child. Amen.

(Light the Advent or Christmas Candles.)

LEADER: My soul magnifies the Lord.

ALL: And my spirit rejoices in God my Savior.

LEADER: For he has looked with favor on the lowliness of his servant.

ALL: Surely, from now on all generations will call me blessed.

LEADER: For unto us is born . . .

ALL: The light and life and hope of the world.

Let someone read the Bible selection for the day. The leader can then read the introductory paragraph for the meditation. Assign two persons to present the lines of dialog involving Mary. The leader can read the concluding thoughts, the reflection question, and brief prayer.

Perhaps members of the group (or family) might bring additional needs and joys to God in prayer, remembering especially anyone who is ill, lonely, or suffering any kind of pain during this season.

The leader can then offer the following blessing:

> *Bless our group (our home) with faith and joy, and hold us close so, like Mary, we may show within us your Word of Life and Love, Jesus Christ. Amen.*

Mary's Magnificat

Let Mary's song of praise be yours this Advent and Christmas
season:

> My soul magnifies the Lord,
> and my spirit rejoices in God
> my Savior,
> for he has looked with favor on
> the lowliness of his servant.
> Surely, from now on all
> generations will call me
> blessed;
> for the Mighty One has done
> great things for me,
> and holy is his name.
> His mercy is for those who fear him
> from generation to generation.
> He has shown strength with his arm;
> he has scattered the proud in
> the thoughts of their hearts.

He has brought down the
powerful from their thrones,
and lifted up the lowly;
he has filled the hungry with good things,
and sent the rich away empty.
He has helped his servant Israel,
in remembrance of his mercy,
according to the promise he made
to our ancestors,
to Abraham and to his
descendants forever.

—Luke 1:46-55

Conversations with Mary

Luke 1:26-33

Mary Accepts

I see Mary trembling when she hears the announcement that she is pregnant. She heard the angel say, "Mary, do not be afraid." I see Mary astonished, shaking, bowing her head, pondering and softly saying, "Yes, God. Yes."

You're scared?
> *I'm just a girl, not expecting a baby at all.*

The angel says you're to be a mother.
> *That's why I'm shaking so. I'm fourteen.*

But others have babies at fourteen.
> *Did you hear the angel? This is no ordinary birth,*
> *no ordinary baby in me.*

Does that make you special?
> *That's why I said "Yes" to Gabriel.*

Because you'll be special?
> *Because the baby is special. The baby will make others*
> *special. It's not just to be my child.*

You'll be seen as different, by Joachim, your father, and Anna, your mother.

> *By all mothers and fathers. This can make me different.*
> *God's son is in me.*

Having this baby in you makes a difference, for you.

> *For anyone. To embrace this baby will make anyone different.*

That's why you're trembling?

> *And that's why I'm saying "Yes" to Gabriel.*

Because you're to be the mother of Messiah.

> *Because Messiah is in me.*

He's yours?

> *I'm his.*

Mary embraced the message; she embraced the baby. She accepted the announcement as something God would do in her, and through her. God's word was alive in her.

What if we thought of ourselves as bearing Christ in us?

O God, how often we invite you to live in us. Make your life in us real, so like Mary we feel your presence within, and carry you full term to others. Amen.

Mary Embraces

I see Mary embracing Gabriel's message with a struggle. She is quizzing Gabriel, but her closing words are, "So be it."

I see a bead of perspiration on your face.
It is a tear.

You have been struggling.
With God's angel.

Over what?
I asked, "How could this great thing come to me?"

The child only needs a mother. You can be that mother.
But this child is Immanuel.

Every mother must ask, "Am I worthy of this little one in me?"
I am young, fragile. And this child is "God with us."

So you debated with God.
I struggled. I asked why and how.

God won.
We won. I will bear the child of God so that all will do it.

All are to embrace this Jesus?

All can make room inside themselves.

All mothers?

All fathers and mothers, sisters and brothers. All can embrace Jesus.

That is what you and the angel debated?

We debated who can carry Christ. Who is worthy to be mother of Jesus. None of us really is.

But you have made room for God in you.

We have this room for God.

Where is this room?

Inside us all.

You mean in the heart. Like the invitation, "Come into my heart, Lord Jesus."

Come in us, among us, through us.

Jesus inside Mary is a miracle. This is the miracle we want inside ourselves—the presence of the person of Jesus.

Where do you need to make room for Jesus to dwell within you?

O God, by your grace, move us to embrace you and carry you to others. Amen.

Mary Walks

I see Mary walking on a high wire. She was promised that she could do the walk and she feels she can. Someone who knows this walk trusts her to do it. She walks on the high wire as though it's a straight white marking on a highway. There is a net to catch her if she falls. She is not afraid of falling. She feels safe.

You're walking where no one has ever walked.
It's a new journey. Gabriel told me the direction I am to go.

The standards for being a mother are high. It won't be easy.
It's a high road. It has to do with the one on high.

You know how far it is down there?
I don't look down there. I don't need to look there to walk.

But it is far down.
I don't look there because that's not where I'm walking.

When you're walking up here, where are you looking?
To the one who believes I can walk here.

You don't think about falling?

I think about the God who believes I can walk here, that I can do it.

It seems very far down.

I am close to the one who believes in me. Gabriel, my mother Anna, my cousin Elizabeth, Joseph, my dearest friend, the prophets, they all keep me looking ahead.

Then you don't look down.

That's not where the child and I are going. We're walking on a high road.

Mary heard news from on high. From Gabriel outlining her life, a birth, the Christ Child she would bear and mother. This was not an ordinary walk of life. What Mary knew to keep her balance was keeping her eyes focused on the one who called her to this walk.

Think about who keeps you on the "high road."

O God, hold me in a way so I feel I do the walking, and help me remember your net of forgiveness is there to catch me if I fall. Amen.

DECEMBER 4
Matthew 1:1, 16-17
John 1:1
Revelation 1:8

Mary Returns

For Mary, believing is like walking in the middle of a strange path. The path is moving from behind her and toward her. The destination of the path of believing seems to be far inside Mary.

You seem to be going somewhere, Mary.
I'm not going. I am coming to somewhere.

Isn't that backwards?
Coming back is where I'm going. I'm always coming back home.

I thought believing meant going somewhere.
Believing is also going back to where I came from.

To your mother's womb? To Anna?
Even farther back.

Are you there now?
I'm always there. Then I go away, and believing brings me back.

Is that how you believe? Is that the way?

My way is recorded. It is my genealogy, and the genealogy of the child in me.

You go back to David.

We go back to the beginning.

In the beginning was God.

That is the beginning where I am going.

That is called the Alpha and Omega.

That is my picture of believing. I live within the Alpha and Omega.

Then faith is in you.

God is in me. Behind me. Before me. Ahead of me.

Believing is a longing for home. Birds migrate with a homing instinct in them. They risk their lives to follow the impulse placed there in creation. We have a "homing device," the Holy Spirit, who guides us home, through the way of believing.

When do you most long for "home"?

O Jesus, our Alpha and Omega, our beginning and end, walk with us and bring us truly home. Amen.

Genesis 1:1-4
John 1:1-5

Mary Beams

I see Mary beaming. She embraced the words of the angel with delight. It was as if she had won a prize. To think she would be mother of the Messiah.

Your face is radiant. You look like you've been in bright sunlight.

It often happens in a mother. We glow.

Is it the chemistry of the body that makes you glow?

It is more. It is the child. The child will be a light in the world.

In the beginning was light. It is recorded in Scripture.

The child is that light. That light from the beginning is in me. So I am glowing.

Rubens will paint the glow around you. Raphael and Michelangelo will paint light surrounding you and the child.

The light is from the child inside. The child is full of light.

The child makes you glow.

The child will be called the Light of the world.

The child in you is living in darkness in you.

The child is light and will shine in darkness. Darkness will not put out the life and light of this child.

Paint brushes and sacred choirs will make your clothing shine, and will adorn your head with halos.

The child will make my spirit glow. And you, too, will reflect that light.

When we embrace Jesus we embrace a light, power, brightness. Jesus is the light and power of God, a glory that changes the whole person. Jesus is the light from light, very God from very God, to us and in us. No darkness or fear or doubt can put out this light.

Remember the brightest word you hear today.

O God, today show us light in some darkness we have. Amen.

Mary Is Held

I see God holding Mary, and Mary being held as a child. As Mary feels God's hug, she passes it on to the baby inside her. God holds us safe, so we can hold another. God holds on to us as a good mother holds her child.

God is holding you.
> *Embracing me. I feel the touch.*

It was not your idea to have a child?
> *I received the message and accepted. God gives me my trust.*

God gave you the miracle without your even asking.
> *I feel God is asking me.*

Asking you to have a baby?
> *And asking me to have faith. God wants me to have God's faith.*

So you think God has faith and God gives faith?
> *Both. God believes in me.*

God has faith.
> *God is faithful. God gives this faith to me. I get to trust God's faith.*

That's why you are embracing the child?
Faith begins with being held, embraced.

How do you know this?
God knows. That's how God began with me.

God believes. God embraces.
Therefore I believe. So I will embrace the baby. The child will know God's trust.

Mary received God's faith and favor. And she returned God's favor. By faith Mary held Jesus. He grew in wisdom and favor with God. The evangelist says, "We love God who first loved us."

Can you remember how or when you first became aware of God's love for you?

O God, you sent Jesus to embrace us with your very love. Wrap your faith around us and hold us safe in love. Amen.

Mary and Joseph Believe

I see Joseph standing beside Mary, watching over her, at peace, believing the angel. The town is filled with gossip. But Joseph is as certain of this miracle as is Mary.

How long have you known Joseph?

All my life. He is a carpenter in Nazareth, building with wood and stone.

What does he say about your being with child?

He knows what to name the child. Jesus.

How did he pick out the name? Is it in the family?

An angel told Joseph in a dream to name the child Jesus, because the child will save people from their sin.

Then Joseph believes in dreams.

We believe in angels.

You are going to Bethlehem?

Caesar Augustus has a law that requires Joseph to go there to register. We will go there together.

It is a five-day journey.

Joseph knows the way.

There are rumors about you and the child. I'm sure Joseph hears them.

Joseph listens only to what the angel said.

It is not his child.

He knows. It will be the child of all the people, to save them. That is enough for Joseph, and for me.

To have faith when others think we are fools to believe in what God is doing in our lives—that is the kind of strong faith Joseph demonstrated.

Think about someone you know who exhibits faith like Joseph's.

O God, give us the peace that comes with believing. Amen.

Mary Grieves

I see Mary quiet, absolutely still, knowing her child has a hard way ahead. Her grief is mixed with joy; her son will be born the Messiah.

You are looking into the distance.
> *The distance is inside me. I am looking into the child in me. Into the child's future.*

You believe in fortune telling.
> *I believe in prophecy. A prophet looks in all directions.*

What do you hear when you look back?
> *Micah the prophet. Isaiah, Jeremiah, Joel, Hannah. I hear their words read in the synagogue.*

Their words have to do with the child in you.
> *Yes. And with the babies inside all mothers.*

What do you hear when you look around?
> *I see armies of Herod, of Caesar, of Egypt. I hear army feet, metal on metal.*

They have to do with your child.
> *With all children. Children are born into a world of battles and metal on metal.*

What do you see when you look ahead?
> *My child will be in battle.*

You want your child to enlist.
> *Children are enlisted before birth. They are in battle when born.*

Gasping for their first breath.
> *Trying to keep their lives. Mine will show them how to live.*

That's why you're looking up.
> *I'm looking up, where peace begins and is completed.*

Your child will bring that peace.
> *That is the prophecy. It gives hope to every mother.*

We inherit a world of warfare, anger, hostility. But through his cross, Christ breaks down the walls of hostility between us, and gives us peace.

Where, how, are you a peacemaker?

O God, in a world of war there was also a world of grace waiting for us at birth. Thank you for making this grace our inheritance. Amen.

Mary Sings

I see Mary with her eyes closed, singing an old love song she heard in her home. She hears lyrics read from the synagogue scroll and she believes the words of the singer. This old song was first a song of Hannah.

It sounds like country music.

> *It is country music, my country's song.*

You made it up.

> *I learned it by heart, the way girls learn songs they hear and like and need.*

You're a musician.

> *A girl can sing when she needs to, when her heart's in it.*

Your song's a hit in the world, high on the charts for centuries.

> *Sometimes a story line fits everyone.*

It's been translated into all languages.

> *I sang it in our little house. My mother heard me.*

You could have been a famous singer. The song caught on in the world.

It doesn't belong to me. It was given to me. By Hannah. It was born inside her. It was reborn in me. It is a song handed down.

Who holds the copyright?

The song belongs to us all; it is in the public domain.

It is called "The Magnificat."

I know. My soul magnifies the Lord!

Some songs live on and on. They do not quit. In Mary's song we find lyrics like some contemporary songs—about love, hope, loneliness, struggle, tears, joy. Every child deserves a song by which to enter and to travel the earth. Because of Jesus, we are all given a magnificent song.

What song or hymn best expresses what God has done for you?

O God, waken in me a theme song, a song I can sing by heart, from the heart. Amen.

Mary Visits

Those who believe need not rehearse their speech of faith. Believing has its own way of speaking.

Where have you been?
> *Up north visiting Elizabeth and Zechariah. She is with child.*

Were you surprised?
> *I surprised her. She opened the door and saw I was pregnant. I told her, but she already knew.*

Did she approve?
> *I have never been so greeted by any relative. She spoke in poetry, each word filled with God's Spirit.*

Then she was glad to see you.
> *Glad to see the child in me. Her baby leaped inside her. Elizabeth shook.*

With excitement?
> *Elizabeth shook with joy. Her baby greeted us.*

Two unborn second cousins met each other in the Spirit.
> *She blessed me. She called me most blessed of women.*

For having this child in you.
  Yes. And for believing.

Believing the angel.
  *She blessed me for believing God's promise to me. The angel is God's
  messenger. I believed the message.*

How did you respond to Elizabeth?
  I sang "the Magnificat" by heart.

It's an old song; Elizabeth knows the words.
  She let me sing it by myself.

You stayed three months. What did you do?
  What I just told you. We sang; we blessed; we laughed.

What did you like best?
  The believing. Together.

There are many ways to see and hear faith. There is a work of
faith, a look of faith, there are songs of faith. But best is a faith
shared together.

Bless someone silently or aloud today.

O God, teach me the art of hospitality when someone comes to
visit me. Amen.

Mary Holds

I see Mary embracing the message of God to herself and holding it tight, hugging the promised child and, at the same time, letting the child go.

When the child is born you'll hold the baby tight?
With my whole body. I'll wrap myself around the baby.

To keep it?
To give him room to grow. I want to give him everything good I have received.

How will you give your child freedom?
I'll hold him with my fingertips.

Why with fingertips?
It's where my energy is released. I want to empower the child.

To empower?
And to release the child.

So you won't hang on?
I'll try to let go, to stay connected to the child through my fingertips.

Like Michelangelo, one finger touching creation.

There's something warm and strong at fingertips. In them a mother and father feel a flame, fire.

A spark. A power.

A connection, a relationship. We leave each other and we keep coming back to each other.

You feel a pull, a magnetism. The child will be magnetic.

People will come to see him. The child will draw others near, to notice, to behold.

And they will see you, the mother.

The child will help those who come near to see all mothers and fathers, children, nations.

Awesome.

Holding a child is awesome. And so is letting go.

Someday the child will embrace you.

I feel the embrace already.

Who held you in a good way when you were little?

O God, how did you decide to hold us by letting us go? Thank you for touching our lives so that we want to keep coming back to you. Amen.

December 12
Luke 1:39-44
Psalm 30:11-12

Mary Dances

I see Mary dancing. She is filled with feelings of ecstasy. A dream coming true has opened up her senses, her soul, completely. She knows what it is to be a girl, woman, mother, prophet. She is conscious of a profound fulfillment within herself. There is new life in her, and she dances with the unborn child.

What does the child feel like in you?
> *A rhythm. A beat.*

Kicking?
> *Like constant ocean waves strong against a shoreline.*

Hitting the sand.
> *Strong and soft. Bare skin against the clean sand.*

He's not hurting you?
> *He's barefoot in me.*

Can you feel the toes pressing?
> *A barefoot dance on a shoreline; dancing barefoot to the tune of tides.*

He's dancing in you?

A barefoot soft-shoe dance. Sliding his way along the edge. The edge of the world. Dancing soft-shoe at the edge of all places he'll go. I am dancing with him. He is my dancing partner.

Why are you bending over?

I am taking off my shoes, to do the barefoot soft-shoe with him.

You know that dance?

The child will teach me.

Will anyone else dance with you?

Mothers are here on the shore. Fathers are here. Ready to dance. They wait at the edge of the world. He will find them here.

They came just to dance?

They live here. He will teach them to dance where they live. In all places along the shoreline, where constant waves smooth out the sand.

The waves erase the footprints of the dance.

They will start over. Whenever he comes, they dance.

They are bowing down.

They are taking off their shoes.

Watch someone dancing in spirit with a child.

O Lord, help me find the child inside me, dancing in motion with your Holy Spirit. Amen.

Psalm 51:10-15
Hebrews 9:28
Hebrews 10:12-17

Mary Offers

I hear Mary singing an old prayer, older than the "Hallelujah Chorus." It is a song sung in the temple of Jerusalem, by a king sorry for his sin. It is a song we sometimes sing as an offertory in church, "Create in me a clean heart, O God."

Everyone knows the song.
> *Everyone. Even the children.*

We often sing it when we bring the offering to God.
> *My child is my offering.*

You mean you are singing an offertory and thinking of the child.
> *The child is the gift I will bring.*

I thought God is giving the child as a gift to you.
> *I will return the gift to God.*

You want the child to be God's.
> *And mine—God's and mine.*

You get it, give it up, and get it back?
> *Yes. All the time, every day. It comes back blessed. The mark will be on the child. The mark of God's name.*

So the child is God's.
> *And mine. Together.*

This song is what keeps you close to God.
> *Close to God. And to the child.*

It is David's song.
> *Yes. And my song.*

For your unborn child.
> *And for me.*

The child will sing it.
> *The child will bring it to pass, making hearts clean and spirits new.*

The mark of God's name is on us through baptism. Like David, we know the need to return to God for a new start when we mess up—and then, forgiven, to offer ourselves again for God's service, in Christ's name.

See everything you have as belonging to yourself and to God.

O God, lift us up, bless us, consecrate us as your own. Amen.

DECEMBER 14
Luke 1:67-79
Luke 22:13-20

Mary Prepares

I see Mary whispering the name "Jesus" and thinking what the name will mean for her child. She knows the Messiah will help people see into their own hearts. As prophets were stoned and rejected, so her son will be. Still she smiles.

What are you preparing? Is that your dinner?
  Salt water and parsley.

Is that part of your diet?
  It is for the Passover. It is part of the meal.

Then it has nothing to do with your pregnancy, or with the child in you?
  It has everything to do with the child in me. Salt water and parsley is about the world into which my child will be born.

What kind of world will it be?
  A world of salt water and tears, of parsley and joy. Those are the worlds my child will know. Tears and joy.

How can you be so sure?

He will be the redeemer. We will name him Jesus, because he will save.

What has that to do with salt water?

He will save people from tears. He will save people from anger and fear and hatred and war.

You mean he will stop all these?

He will lead people through these. In the midst of all these, and at the end of all these, he will bring people joy.

Joy is the parsley?

Joy is the green springtime, the new life after winter. My child will bring life in the middle of death.

Then you are glad to give him this birth?

I have more parsley than salt water. Joy will outlive tears.

Jesus leaves us with a meal of joy: the Eucharist, his own body and blood.

What brings you joy? To whom can you bring joy today?

O God, give us joy and hope that exceeds all hurt and harm. Keep our eyes on good that overcomes evil. Amen.

Mary Sees

Mary knows that leaders are followed or hated, adored or despised, believed or scorned, embraced or rejected. How will the world see her son?

You are looking into the future. And yet you look like you're all alone.

> *I'm not alone. Most of the people I know are also looking into the future.*

What does the future look like to you?

> *My child to come is my future. That is the future I see.*

When is the baby due?

> *Soon.*

When the child is born will you have seen your future?

> *That's when the future takes a new turn. That's when the future will be in person, in Jesus.*

There will be something to do in the future.

> *There will be someone to follow. We will go into the future following my son. He will lead and we will see the way.*

How will we see the way?
>*He will be the Way.*

What does that mean?
>*It means we will look to see the way he is.*

What will keep us in this way, his way?
>*His truth.*

Then he will be called the Way and the Truth?
>*And the Life.*

For three days, some children and I looked at Jesus as "the Way." We studied roads, paths, highways, jet streams, trails, creeks. These were our "way" pictures. When the days were done, the children agreed Jesus is interested most of all in "the way we are," the way Christ's way can be in us.

How is Jesus' way visible in you?

O God, make the life of Christ a way we live with one another. Amen.

Mary Remembers

I see Mary dreaming of when her people were in exile. She hears their songs of homeland, and feels their homesick spirit. Her hope is that the child within her will bring joy to her nation.

You seem a little homesick.
> *I have never left home.*

But you know about longing for home?
> *I can see the feeling in the eyes of the old people in the synagogue. I know about longing.*

You see it in their eyes?
> *I hear it in their songs, in the voices of their old singers.*

In their psalms.
> *In their spirituals. I know the longing from my family. Elizabeth, Zacharias. Relatives. Ones who sing of old times.*

They know songs from exile. Songs of slavery, injustice.
> *Songs of longing from the hills and riverside of Babylon.*

But you are home.
> *I know Babylon.*

You were never along the river of Babylon.
> *We don't only live where we are.*

The child in you hears your song.
> *The child hears the songs of exile.*

The child will make music?
> *Waken music. He will waken music on highways, along rivers, in cotton fields, concert halls, in prisons.*

Everything wants to sing. Everyone.
> *And to come home. To come home, at last.*

Ancestors give us their songs, their stories, their hopes. We inherit places we have never been. And on our own, we have experienced exile and captivity. Heaven is painted in the Scriptures as home. Jesus is the one who brings us there.

When or how have you felt you were in exile or captivity?

Thank you, God, for bringing us, through exile, back "home" to you. Amen.

December 17

John 1:14, 181
Corinthians 13:12-13
Hebrews 1:1-5

Mary Expects

I see a child about to be born who knows the mystery of heaven, of eternity. This child is not only of the mother but is also of God. Compressed inside this infant is the mind, power, and kingdom of God. Even as history is compressed inside a molecule of DNA, so in this one is held all the attributes and nature of God.

What are you expecting?
A miracle.

Dark hair? Brown eyes? What do you hope for?
A miracle. This one is of God.

God packed inside a newborn?
This is how God looks when born an infant.

He'll sleep like all babies. He'll have to learn to walk and talk.
That's the miracle. God joins our life completely. God wants us to see God in the world.

To see the baby.
> *To see God. In this baby we will see God.*

Is that as close as we get to God?
> *This is as close as God gets to us. In Jesus.*

To see the baby is like looking at God.
> *It is as close as God will get to us.*

Surely God can get closer to us.
> *Not yet. This is the best way for us to see now. With our eyes.*

You will be the mother of God.
> *I believe Gabriel. This baby in me is God in human form.*

A baby who will be important.
> *God is important. That is what the baby is showing us.*

The Council of Nicea looked at the nature of Jesus, and agreed. Jesus is fully of God, and is fully human. In this birth we see God appearing.

What do you know about God from looking at Jesus?

O God, in the excitement of every birth and new life, let us also see your presence. Amen.

December 18
Exodus 2:1-10; 15:19-21

Mary Tells

I see Mary ready to wrap her newborn into cloth, to fold it tight around to make the baby safe. In Nazareth she learned to wrap swaddling cloths. Now she is in Bethlehem, far from home, ready to make her newborn doubly safe.

You are a protective mother.
> *I am making sure the child will be safe.*

You know how to wrap the child; your mother taught you?
> *I watched the mothers, my neighbors.*

You are alone here in Bethlehem.
> *No mother is really alone. There is Joseph and there are other mothers and fathers. Someone will help if I ask.*

Will you let others hold the child?
> *First a mother wants to hold the newborn. After a while many will hold the child; they'll wrap him and rock him.*

Your lips are moving.
> *I'm reciting stories to tell the child.*

The child is too young to hear these stories.

For nine months I have whispered these stories.

Stories for children?

About children. Water stories. The story of Moses in the water, and Miriam his sister keeping watch over the baby.

What other stories are you whispering?

The story of the ark rocking in the storm, safe in the flood. I will hold my child tight to me when I tell this story.

Any other water stories?

I will whisper the story about the children crossing the sea.

Your child will learn that story?

Those who crossed the Red Sea to safety are my relatives. Miriam is a distant relative of my child.

She danced.

One day in Cana my child will dance with me.

A child made safe and secure is learning to dance. We, through baptism, are made part of the water stories. Made safe. And prepared to dance.

Who knows safety and security because of you?

O God, teach me the joy of your salvation, and to dance! Amen.

Micah 5:2
Isaiah 11:1-2, 6
John 15:26-27

Mary Believes

Mary's believing is like a fine spider web. It is thin, it is strong. A web is born from within a spider, yet the web can hold the spider. Mary had a faith that was born of God from inside her. It could carry more than her weight.

What does believing look like?
  It is a thin thread inside me.

Where does it begin?
  I know it is tied to my mother. I know the thread of believing that is in her.

One end is tied to your mother?
  It extends beyond my mother, to generations before her.

You cannot see it, but you feel it is there.
  I know it is there. It is not just her word. She heard the word from God.

Can you hear it?
  Sometimes the word makes the sound of a song, as of a wind. It is often an old psalm.

Do you hear it here in Bethlehem?

David played the song in the hills here, with the sheep.

Can I hear the sound?

When you believe, the word can sound like a song.

The Spirit can help my belief?

God's Spirit is like wind, with a story that can sing.

You learned this from your mother.

It is deep inside me.

You are attached to it.

Faith holds me. It is my strength and support.

Believing is a gift of the Spirit to us, in us, and through us. By faith, we become attached to a story line that began before our birth and extends far beyond us.

How is believing passed along in your family?

O God, keep me attached to the story of Jesus, and make my believing like a string, taut at two ends, held strong by you. Amen.

Mary Awaits

Mary and Joseph are away from home. But Mary's mind is full of wonder. She has brought a child to its due date.

You're getting things ready.
> *It's time.*

You've been counting the days.
> *Centuries. Our people, all of us, have been counting the centuries.*

It doesn't take that long to have a baby. Not centuries.
> *We have waited for centuries. Prophets have predicted the coming. Mothers hoped their child would be the one.*

So this is the one.
> *This is the one. The time has come.*

You don't mean just the nine months.
> *I mean the fullness of time has come.*

When did that time begin?
> *When the promise was conceived.*

When Gabriel appeared to you in Nazareth?

Before. The promise God made to our fathers and mothers, to Abraham and Sarah, to Adam and Eve.

That's when they began to count the days?

To count generations, lifetimes, the years, the minutes.

How will you celebrate the birth? With balloons and cigars and flowers?

Just with his name. We'll call him Immanuel.

But what will you use to celebrate?

Immanuel is the celebration.

It means "God with us."

God is with us. That is the excitement. The child is the celebration.

Each birth makes a difference, each newborn changes the universe. Mary's child, Jesus, makes all the difference in the world. In Christ, God is with us in all we go through.

Who counted the days waiting for your birth? Hold them in prayer.

O God, thank you for those who were there at my birth, there at my early life, who helped me know your presence, too. Amen.

Luke 1:30-33
John 3:1-8
Isaiah 9:6-7

Mary Ponders

I see Mary awed. She is pondering her conception. What does it mean to conceive of the Holy Spirit? How will the child inside her be a part of her and a part of God? How shall he be recorded in the census of Caesar? To whom will he belong?

The child is of God.
> *It is not as I ever thought. Sarah and Hannah wanted a child. Each had a husband. Their children had fathers.*

Your child is of the Spirit.
> *Of God. He will always be in Abba's house. He will not always be my own. He will know his genealogy.*

How will you get his mind on earth?
> *He will know the will of Abba in heaven and Abba's will on earth.*

Will it be easy to keep him homebound, in your kingdom?
> *He will know about his birth; Joseph will tell him about the dreams. I will take him to springs, and we will walk along the sea, through green pastures, to crossroads where east and west highways meet.*

That will keep his mind on earth.

> *He will see crowds of rich and sick and poor. He will hear lepers and blind begging. I will watch him. He will do Abba's will on earth. He will keep my mind here also.*

You will watch him be on earth.

> *And I will watch him be in heaven. He will know Abba's will in heaven. The child also will keep my mind on heaven. Since he came into me, my mind is on Abba. That is his home; it is my inheritance.*

Is it that way with all children, in their mothers?

> *I will inherit my child's lineage, his future and past. We pass our legacy to one another. We keep it for each other, deep inside.*

Your son will give you his inheritance.

> *He will give his legacy to all. He is of Abba; he is of flesh. This is what we all inherit.*

Mary, you have your mind set on earth and on heaven.

> *Both will be in the mind of my child. It is what we all inherit. Being of Abba and of a mother.*

Look at a single article of faith—at what it holds of heaven and what it holds of earth. And marvel.

O God, how very much we are born of your heaven and of your earth. Amen.

Mary Adores

Adoration is looking into the eyes of another, wondering what all the other person is and knows. Adoration is being overwhelmed by the mystery of someone you love.

You're looking down to the child in you.
> *He is my only son.*

Are you nearsighted? Your eyes are so close.
> *I am really farsighted.*

You're an inch away from him.
> *I'm not only looking at him. I'm looking at his future. And I'm looking at his past.*

How can you see both ways at once?
> *In him I see everything past and what is to come.*

How do you know his past?
> *We are all part of his history. His story. He is from the beginning.*

Then we're in him.
> *What he has we need. He will give us whatever we need.*

He will take us from the past into our future.

>*Into his future.*

Then we are to live in him?

>*I am in him; he is in me.*

He is your unborn child.

>*I will stay close to see where we will go, together.*

What do you call what you are doing?

>*Adoration. Longing to be where he is, and was, and will be.*

When we look into the face of a newborn, we look back to the child's inheritance and we look ahead with expectation. We look at the Christ Child the way lovers keep looking at each other, remembering and hoping.

Think about belonging to another person's future. And to God's.

O Christ, you have come so we can see you and one another. Now we see in part, but we see. Help us adore you here until we see you face to face. Amen.

DECEMBER 23
Galatians 4:4-5
Romans 8:22-29

Mary Keeps Time

I see Mary sitting by the Sea of Galilee. She hears the water splashing against the shore, thinks of the beauty of strong tidal waves, keeping time with the universe, like the rhythm of a clock. That is what I imagine in her mind, as her labor begins.

So you've all been waiting.

We always wait together. No one waits alone.

For the child.

The child in me waits, I wait, and all those around me wait. We wait together.

You're breathing in rhythm.

The child helps us breathe together.

You're looking out there somewhere.

In there, where the child lives. We're all looking at the child, listening to the beat of his heart.

To a child whom you can't see.

Not yet. That's why we're looking. And counting.

Counting helps the pain. Counting helps keep the breathing in rhythm. It hurts to give birth. To wait.

Waiting when you can't see what you're waiting for can hurt.

Watching the clock helps.

We always watch the big hand.

Is the hand moving to twelve?

To the fullness of time.

When is the fullness of time?

The child knows.

You're smiling. You said it hurt, and you're smiling.

The child is coming.

There is a time for everything. Sometimes we know that time, just after it comes. It is not a time we plan. It comes with the birth of a miracle. It comes especially with the miracle of God making time for us. And loving us through Christ, for time and eternity.

Listen to what people you know wait and hope for most.

O God, thank you for entering time and space in Jesus, for us to know our salvation. Amen.

Mary Sees Light

W onder is to experience something so great we can't take it all in. We have to look away, and remember. It's too much to see at once.

You're squinting.
It's too bright.

The sun isn't shining. It's night.
What I'm looking into isn't sunlight.

What are you seeing?
What's happening now, in me. I'm finally seeing it.

After all these months.
After all these centuries. I'm finally seeing it tonight.

Where are you?
Here in Bethlehem. This night, the glory of the Lord is shining.

That's what we read in Luke. We read about God's glory.
That's what I'm seeing. It's so bright a light.

It's like a Christmas play when I was a child.
This is no play. This light is for real.

Where's the light coming from?

From on high; from inside; from all around.

It's dark, and you see a great light?

I see the glory the shepherds saw. The good news.

You see the words written in the Bible.

I see the word which is my own flesh and which dwells in me.

That is overwhelming.

I am filled with wonder.

Saul was blinded when he met Jesus on the road. He saw a light that transformed him. The light of Jesus is what transforms us daily. We can see like new. We finally catch on. We finally hear angels of Bethlehem even in our home town. We can finally wonder. We finally see the light.

Where do you see the light of Christ today?

O God, there is too much for us to see. Help us to look reverently. Help us in a glimpse or a glance to see your coming to us again in love. Amen.

Luke 2:7-12
2 Corinthians 8:9

Mary Gives Birth

I see Mary giving birth to Jesus in a stable. How can a king be born in hay? How does Mary feel about giving birth in a cattle stall?

Mary, your child is born. But in a cattle shed?
>*Straw is his bed. He has a place to lay his head. It will be but for a little while. He may never own a house. Not many own their own place.*

You're glad for this cattle stall?
>*There is no other place. Besides, he is born for all creation. He is the first fruit of all creation.*

There is a report of angels appearing to shepherds on the hillside.
>*They can find the child here. This is a common place they may visit.*

Shepherds would need a permit to see your child in a castle.
>*He is born for all to see. "He will scatter the proud in the thoughts of their hearts . . . He will fill the hungry with good things." I sang this in the house of Elizabeth and Zechariah.*

"The Magnificat" gives us a clue?

Yes. That it is right for the birth of Jesus to be here.

Then you did not expect a castle for his birthplace?

No. It is in my song. He will bring "down the powerful from their thrones" and "lift up the lowly."

"God so loved the world." Whether our beginnings are humble or noble, the Christ Child desires to make his home with us.

What one thing could you do to "lift up the lowly" this Christmas?

O God, make where I am a place where all can kneel and worship you. Amen.

Isaiah 60:1-3
John 12:32-33
Luke 7:20-23

Mary Invites

They will come from all ends of the earth. All nations will be drawn to this child.

Mary, he will be famous.
> *He will make all who come see him famous.*

You are near a field of sheep.
> *If shepherds come to worship, they will leave this place running with gladness. They will come to see the Lamb and leave with a new song.*

If kings and queens were to come?
> *They would surely bring him gifts of silver and gold. They would leave some treasure and take him home treasured in their hearts.*

If lepers came?
> *He'd reach out to touch them. They'd go home healed, rejoicing.*

What if the blind came to see the child? Would they find him?
> *He'd guide them with his voice. He'd call them by their name. They would go home with new hope, new vision.*

Mary, what if Herod came to see him?

Herod or other kings cannot destroy this child. They will leave believing he is dead. But he will rise. And he will look for them, that they, too, might see him, believe, and live.

What if I could come to see the Christ Child?

You can. Come now.

In a Bethlehem stable, God holds open house for all people, of all times.

What draws you to Jesus?

O God, thank you for drawing the whole world to yourself. Help me be part of your drawing power. Amen.

Luke 2:13-20

Shepherds Adore

I see Mary showing her child to the shepherds. She is letting them come close. They kneel to look closer at the child as though they are reading the very word of God.

Mary, the shepherds are coming close to the child. A newborn can catch a disease.

They need to be as close as possible. The shepherds need this proof.

Glory covers them.

God's glory draws glory out of the shepherds.

That's why you let them come so close?

They will be people of glory, people of light.

They may breathe on the child's face.

Believing is about being close. They will want to see and touch what they believe. They will want to feel the child breathe, to be sure there is life.

So you'll not be embarrassed by the odor of their clothes, by their matted hair?

Believing is about the inside, not the outside.

They won't know how to be reverent.
They will know. They will worship in a cattle stall.

Who will lead their worship?
The child. The child knows all the parts by heart.

They'll come running, stop in silence, and bow down.
That is worship. Adoration.

They'll tell the story of the good news; they'll all talk at once.
Telling good news is worship.

They will feast their eyes on the child. They will find their proof in the hay.
That is God's way. To come where we least expect it.

In worship we come to adore, to feast our eyes on the one who came for shepherds and lost sheep.

What is different in your life because you have felt the breath of Christ on you?

O God, thank you that we can come close to you just as we are. Amen.

Mary Looks

I see Mary looking for a moment at the world into which her child will be born. In her youth she has heard stories of Herod's cruelty. In Galilee and on her long walk to Bethlehem, she has seen Roman soldiers, has felt the occupation. Mary believes her child knows a kingdom more powerful than Roman garrisons, mightier than Herod's evil forces.

Mary, how is it to bring a child into Herod's world?

It is not Herod's world. This is the world of Abba, the one in heaven.

Herod will not like this child who is to rule, to have glory.

It is not Herod's kingdom. He rules for only a while. There will be other Herods, and they will be forgotten. His house will wash into the sand.

Your child will be a threat to royal powers. Soldiers will be ordered against little ones.

It will always be so. There will be heavy boots marching down side streets to the houses of other children, to steal life from cradles, to pillage playgrounds.

Why do you bring a child into this world?

> *There is no other world. There is no world without a Herod. Yet, this is not Herod's world. Remember: Hosts of angels unfolded the heavens. Glory shone around. They sang of peace in Herod's day. It is my child's world.*

The word is out. Herod's armies are coming in this direction.

> *While children can hear Herod coming, my Joseph hears Gabriel, who knows more than the military. Angels take away our fear of Herods. Angels know more than intelligence departments of kings.*

Where is Joseph?

> *He is gathering our possessions, and the child. We will flee to be safe.*

But you will all be refugees. This is no way for a child to live.

> *That is how many begin life. The long line that flees in the night.*

Mary, are you afraid?

> *The angel said, "Be not afraid." We believe. The message is from God.*

When will you return?

> *When Herod is dead. The child will outlive Herod and his kingdom.*

Focus on the destiny of a child you know. See in that destiny the rule of God's peace and love.

O God, help us remember the power and longevity of good heroes. Amen.

Mary Weeps

I see Mary leading a funeral dirge. There are tears, sobs, whimpering, shouts. It sounds like a choir of random voices, clashing tones, without melody. Still it is their music. Mary is leading the cries of all mothers who weep, who have no control, whose voices reflect violence against them.

You sound off key.
> *There is no key. We each sing in our own key.*

It sounds like modern music.
> *It's old, ancient music. From the beginning of time.*

Who is in this procession?
> *Rachel, who died in childbirth. But there is so much weeping in the world. Many are making music.*

I can't catch all the words being sung.
> *They are lamentations.*

You know all the words?
> *We have this in common. We sing our sorrow.*

Most don't have sheet music.
> *We know the songs by heart.*

Will you stay in the choir long?
> *Until we don't need the songs we're singing. When the songs are done.*

Where are the children of whom you sing?
> *In Bethlehem, Buchenwald, Bosnia. In Northern Ireland. In Selma and Vietnam. In Rwanda and Flander's Field.*

There are those who know how to sing against and through injustice. They make sounds that help the world hear what children cannot say loudly enough, children who are too little and too weak. Their lamentations magnify not only the Lord, but the pain of innocent children.

Pay attention to some injustice toward children in our world, and hear the sounds of their suffering.

O God, when we see the innocent suffering, give us a fitting song to sing. Amen.

Mary Forgives

G rief sometimes looks like a spiderweb that catches its prey. The web clings to the prey and it will never let go. Mary's grief was not like this. She grieved for those who would catch Jesus in a web, for she believed her son would outlive the enemy. Her grief was for the enemy, the offender.

You're sad.
> *He'll die early.*

He'll be caught in the crossfire?
> *He's the one they'll set out to capture, to condemn, to kill.*

It'll be an unfair trial.
> *That's why I grieve.*

For the injustice.
> *For their injustice. I grieve for them.*

Your child is the victim.
> *They are the victims. They are the ones hurt. I grieve for them.*

For whom should they grieve?

For themselves. Grief should be a sign of their sorrow.

They will not be punished. For this they will not have to die.

That will be his wish.

That they are to be forgiven?

And that they repent, and that they love.

Your son will be dead.

He will live. If they grieve, and repent, they will live.

His blood will cry out.

The cry will become a song—a Christmas song. And an Easter song.

Good grief is a mourning that need not get even. It washes away the hurt, the retaliation, the anger, and cleanses the wound inside the mind, in the spirit. Grief is part of the healing. Grief and grace can heal a wounded victim.

As this year comes to a close, is there someone you need to forgive or ask forgiveness from?

O God, when they condemned and crucified Jesus, love began—for those beneath the cross, and also for us. Thank you for your love. Amen.

Mary Trusts

I see Mary in a boat with friends. Waves sometimes get high but they are not afraid. They ride the storm laughing, telling stories, and singing. Everyone has brought picnic baskets for a party on board. I know I, too, belong in this boat with these people, and look forward to the sunset and the other shore.

Mary, what are you doing in the boat?
The Sea of Galilee is near my town. We are sailing.

Do you know where you're going?
We are at sea.

Is there a chart plan?
There is. It is with the captain.

This isn't a pirate ship?
We are all friends. We planned this trip for a long time. The captain invited us.

Will there be a storm?
I am not worried. The captain knows the sea. We have all ridden out storms.

What if the waves get high, and you fall into the sea?

There will be someone to help us up. We have all fallen before.

Will there be enough to eat on board?

Plenty. We have each brought something. There is enough. There is always enough.

How safe is the boat?

The captain knows. He made the boat, just for this sea.

Are there other seas?

The captain knows.

In Baptism, we are invited into the trip of a lifetime. The church is a people who are all at sea on a very large pilgrimage. The captain, Christ, will teach us to trust him, the boat, the sea, and each other.

How did your friends, your family, members of your faith help each other ride out life's storms this past year?

O God, keep us in community for our safety and for our believing. Help us enter the new year with less fear—more joy and trust in you. Amen.

January 1
Luke 2:25-32

Mary Glows

A we is to be in the presence of a celebrity, up close. It is not knowing whether we should bow, kneel, or jump for joy. We hold our breath so what's happening won't disappear. We run to tell others. We smile. We just smile, that is all.

You look like you had a vision. Your face is glowing.
What seemed impossible is real. It's right before me.

You didn't think it could happen.
I thought it could happen. I believe in miracles.

Why the glow?
The miracle is still happening, around me.

You are in the center.
The miracle is my center, and my circumference.

You're very special. Lots of people are looking.
They are looking at him, some close up, some from a distance.

The light reaches that far?
This miracle is bigger than the space right around me or them.

The countryside glowed?
> *Shepherds thought night had turned to day. They came running to the child, to adore him.*

And now here in the city? In Jerusalem?
> *Here, too, God's glory is revealed.*

Simeon saw the light.
> *And held him in his arms.*

Awe is recognizing God's miracle come close to us, around us and in us.

Think about what New Year's resolution, what practice, might help you adore Christ more this year.

O God, thank you for coming close to us and letting our eyes, like Simeon's, see your light and salvation. Amen.

Mary Comforts

People are rending their garments, eyes filled with disillusionment. The air is filled with the mourning cries heard in Arab lands when a son or daughter is stoned or shot to death. In this suffering sound I see Mary, staring off into the distance, seeing something hopeful beyond the pain.

They're tearing their clothes.
> *It's like what animals do to stand the pain. Animals sometimes bite into their wounds or into wood.*

What does tearing do to pain?
> *Lets it flow through the body and out. It releases pain.*

Ripping cloth can do that?
> *Pain is a tearing apart.*

The noise of grief is louder than the ripping cloth.
> *A parting sound.*

Of separation.
> *Of a body being broken. My son will hear this sound of grief.*

The sound of crying goes with the tearing of the cloth. They are feeling the pain.

They are letting the grief go. It will be destroyed.

Grief will leave them.

We can hear it in their voices. We can hear it in the ripping of cloth.

Is it finished when the cloth is torn?

The tearing releases the grief. Then comes the peace.

Grief is a rending, a tearing, a weeping, a sobbing time. Grief must leave the body to relieve pain. Then comes the calm, the quiet, and hope is reborn.

Let out pain that is stuck inside, and see it leave.

O God, help us to see that when we think something is finished, it is for you and for us a new beginning. Amen.

Mary Shares

I see mothers giving birth on death beds, in rooms hidden from friends and family, in university hospitals. I see babies born in castles, in cotton fields, in back seats of cars, on fine linen, upon straw. I see Mary giving birth, and birth in all these places.

Where are you going?
> *To the corners of the earth, for a birth.*

Why are we going to these other places?
> *These mothers are in travail. They want a child to bring their earth peace.*

You are going to show the child you bore to these mothers and fathers?
> *It is to be their child, a member of their families.*

Would you want your child to be born in a strange city or village?
> *That is where children are born, known, named, loved—in all these places.*

In Afghanistan?

In Nairobi, Ghana, Bolivia, Beijing, Newcastle, Anchorage, Nebraska.

Your child is a citizen of Judea, recorded on the rolls of Caesar Augustus.

Yes, and a citizen of the whole earth, every city, each slum, each countryside, each tiny village, each place where there is birth.

Wherever babies are counted?

Also where babies are not counted. Where they are born and sold, discarded or destroyed.

This birth is to be waited for and celebrated in all these places.
How will we get to all these places of birth?

We will follow my child.

Jesus came to make us one family. He was born in one place, of one mother. He is a sign of the worth of each child, the worth of each mother and father bringing life to birth.

Look at each child today as Jesus' sister or brother.

O God, bring your honor and dignity to babies born this day. Amen.

Mary Is Surprised

The first sight of a newborn—by mother, father, or grand-parents—should be photographed. For the first look at a newborn is one of pure surprise. So, I believe, it was for Mary.

The child is here.
> *It wasn't there, and now it's here.*

A surprise.
> *I knew it was coming. That is not the surprise.*

Why the surprised look on your face then?
> *It's for me. It's my own. That's the surprise.*

It happens every day.
> *It's the first time for me. My own closest relative.*

That is what you're thinking?
> *I'm not just thinking; I'm feeling this connection.*

What's the feeling?
> *How can one so wonderfully made be mine?*

Your face is full of delight.
I'm full of adoration.

Where did you learn about adoration?
The baby is teaching me to adore.

What's the baby doing?
Letting me hold it.

Why the light on your face?
It's from the baby.

Surprise is to be overwhelmed by goodness. In the moment of surprise I feel on fire. I feel all is calm, all is bright. We get to hold with our own hands one whom we never held before. That is a moment in which to be still.

Think about communion as holding, receiving Christ, into your own hands, surprising you again with his love.

O God, thank you for sending Christ to be our closest relative. Keep our minds open to your surprises this new year. Amen.

Isaiah 35:1-2
John 3:16
I Corinthians 15:20-23

Mary Believes

elieving seems easier when pussy willows bloom, when robins appear, and the earth turns green.

I see the willows are budding. It's that time.
> *It is more than willows opening.*

You mean the trees, the tulips. It's that time of year.
> *It's that time in my life. The baby has come. Everything is coming to life.*

The meadows, the roses of Sharon, the lilies of the valley.
> *I see more than these. I also see the graves blooming.*

The grass, meadows.
> *The saints. I see life in the grave.*

You mean on the grave, the flowers in canisters.
> *I see God's signs of life, with God's verses on the marble stones.*

You believe the Bible verses carved in marble.
> *Yes, I believe. And I believe God's green earth, the violets in bloom, rose moss—they are pictures of faith.*

You believe in flowers.

I believe in God, in God's life, in life everlasting.

Where do you see eternal life?

In the tip of the willow. Spring is only the tip of the iceberg.

You believe in nature?

I believe in the creator of earth.

Of heaven.

I believe in the maker of earth and heaven. And I believe the maker's word. And that word made flesh, in my baby.

Nature highlights God's word in living color. But there is an even clearer word from God, in living color. It is God's Son, who longs to bring all things to life, and conquers even death and the grave.

Touch something in nature intentionally each day, and say, "Thank you, God, I believe."

O God, sometimes I read and believe, sometimes I look to believe, sometimes I wait for a season to come. In the dawn, in the dew, in night watches, help me believe in the abundant life you offer in Christ Jesus. Amen.

Mary Nurses

I see Mary nursing her child. She holds the child, knowing how fragile this new life is, how dependent upon her help. It is her first time to mother. In her mind is the thought that one born of God is at her breast. In an innocent way she perceives the span of him, human and divine. Her child is of God.

Mary, you are so beautiful with the child.

Why have you come?

To paint you, for all the people, who cannot be here, now, or later. I have brought bush and easel.

The child is hungry, and I must feed the thirst.

Feed the child; I will choose soft colors, skin colors. The people will want to see the child at your breast. That is where all the people's children go. All need a mother.

The child is my own. I carried him in me, as all mothers must. I waited, watching the way the child grew, moved, made me walk slowly up to Bethlehem. Now the child cries when thirst sets in. They are not on their own, when born. None can live alone when so little—or ever.

The painting will hang in galleries of Amsterdam and London, in New York City, in Madrid, in San Francisco. Crowds will stand before you, Mary.

The child will go into all the world. Sometimes on foot, sometimes with shepherds, and in countless other ways.

I will paint your dress blue. Millions will know you that way. Generations will memorize the colors.

How will you paint the child?

The color of your breast.

The child does not live only here in Bethlehem. The child sits at the right hand of God.

Mary, for that I have bright gold color. Burning like fire. The halo. The color of divinity, of holiness.

You will paint the gold around the child.

I will paint the gold around you and the child, and Joseph, and all present. It is not only a color for the child.

Gabriel said the same. Simeon promised the child would come to all the people. The child is not only at my breast.

The child is sleeping now. Tomorrow I will bring others with their brushes and easels, to paint what they see.

Where do you live?

In Italy.

The child will wake again. They know when they are hungry. Then you will finish painting.

Mary, what shall I paint as background to you and the child?

Italy. It is where you live. The child will also live in Italy. He will be wherever you live.

Stay with a painting or a song of Mary and child, and wonder at their presence there with you.

O God, show me the depth, height, length, and width of the one born in Bethlehem, and of us all. Amen.

Unto Us Is Born has been slightly revised from its first publication as a booklet of Advent devotions for Wheat Ridge Ministries.

Wheat Ridge Ministries, located in Itasca, Illinois, is a Lutheran organization that helps start new ministries of health and hope around the globe, enabling God's people to care for a broken and hurting world in the name of the healing Christ.

Christmas Prayer

Dear God of power, ages, might,
How came the thought to Thee
To come as infant tiny one
Inside nativity?

How came this willing, gentle girl
To give such heart to Thee
That in her body there did form
All earth's nativity?

Dear God of glory, eons, light,
Creator of us all,
Make me thy manger full of faith
As Mary's cattle stall.

—Herbert Brokering

People to Remember in Prayer